Note to Self
A Meditation in 36 Parts

S. Hunter

Written and illustrated by S. Hunter.

Published by **TITHONUS**

All Enquiries:
TITHONUS
2 Carter Road,
Burwell,
Cambridge.
United Kingdom.
CB25 0DN

Printed and bound in the UK by the MPG Books Group, Bodmin and King's Lynn

ISBN 978-0-9573238-0-3

For Neil, Lewis, Emma, Kerry and Katie.

NOTE
TO
SELF

I. Well ... It All Seems To Be Connected OK ...

Tracing the pathways
Into, out of, through;
Beyond interconnected.

We are all interconnected. Things other people do are transmitted across these interconnecting networks and affect us; sometimes those effects can be very noticeable. In turn, everything we do is transmitted along those very networks with the potential to impact on others. We can only wish that any impact we might have serves to improve our collective interconnected existence.

Be nice and
Do as you would be done by.
This is the only way.

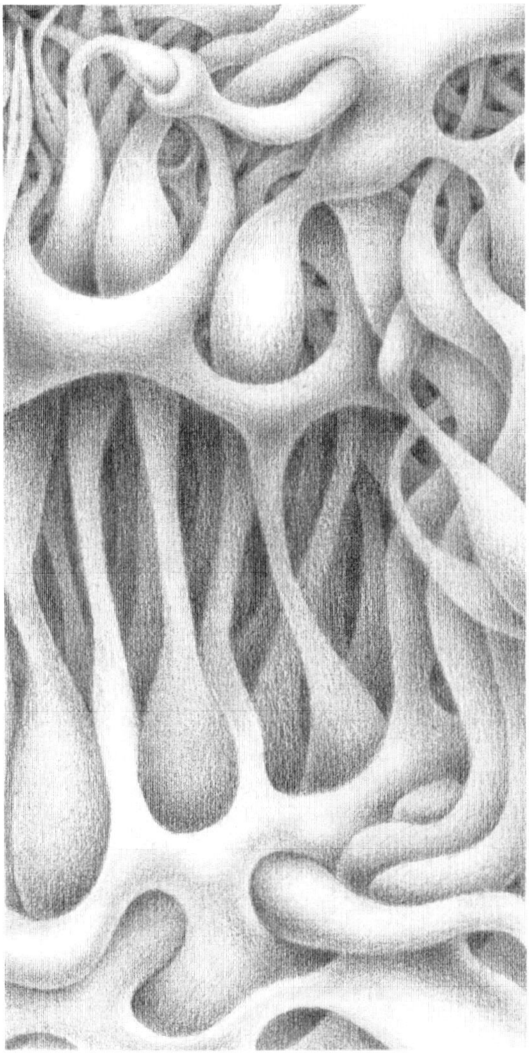

II. Towards The Light

A sunny day;
The company of friends;
The journey is everything.

We are all on the way to somewhere. We may think we are in control but quite often, un-noticed forces are directing our progress.

We are as much a product of luck as conscious choice. Without working towards a goal, we will never achieve our full potential. Without the chances of an opportunity, all our work could be wasted. Who can say what will happen, all we can do is to work at what feels right and follow where the opportunities lead.

III. Dreams And Potentials

Dreaming the dreams,
Planning the plans;
Actions will be required.

We all have dreams and potentials. The trick is to keep them safe against a landscape of ups and downs.

Some people become lost or lose everything. Some people compare themselves to others and feel disappointed. Some people look upon others with a pretence of superiority. Some people just don't care anymore and some become afraid.

The lucky ones learn to take on board all that life can throw and still want to grow, change and face the new day to see what events will unfold.

I hope I'm lucky.

IV. Fast And Bulbous … In Slow Motion

In great haste
Going nowhere fast;
That's normal isn't it?

To sit and watch the sun set; the starlings morphing their way across the sky; the killers on muffled wings looking for rodents. It brings a sense of perspective after the rush of the normal day and sorts out what matters from the trash of modern life.

The universe is an incredibly beautiful place.

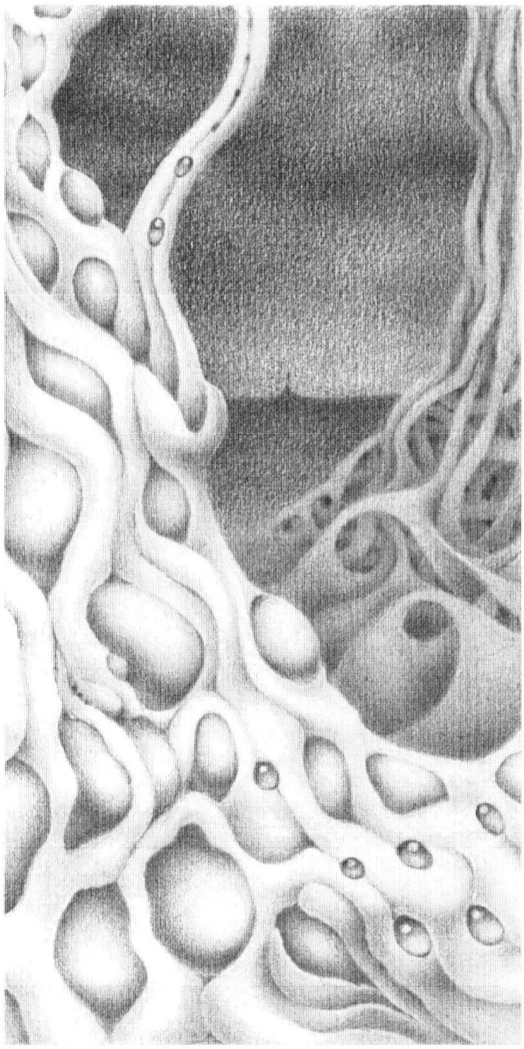

V. The Guardian

Places of privacy;
A guardian keeps the door;
This far and no further.

Some things do not mean well nor do they contribute to any sense of progression or 'goodness'. We all need a guardian to keep the door and stop the nasties. It can be hard to stop the negativity creeping in … best to catch it as soon as possible, reveal it for the foulness it is, then throw it out.

Objective evaluations are extremely rare and incredibly valuable; they are constructive and designed to help improve any endeavour. Too often negativity is thinly veiled as critique. You can always tell the two apart, critique is always well meant.

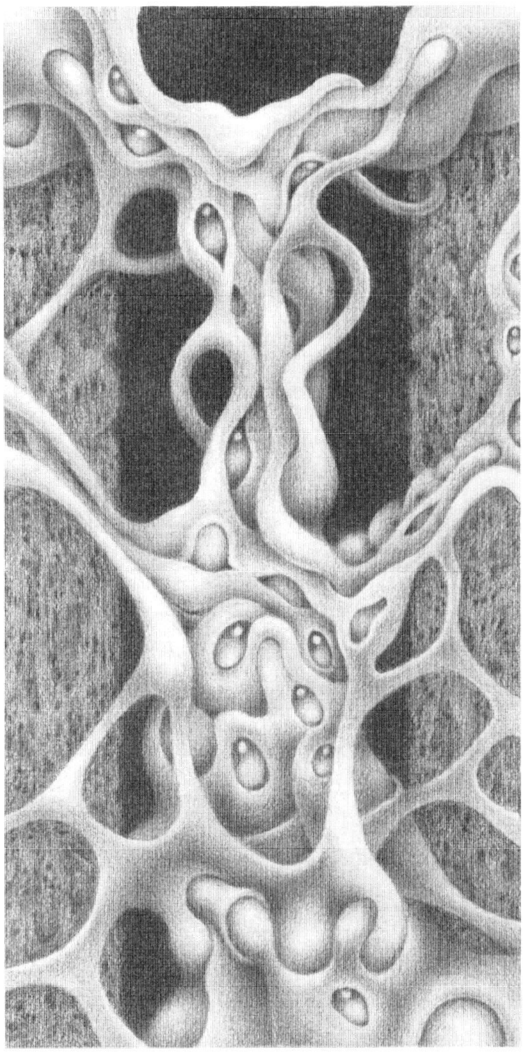

VI. UNCOVERED

This mature content
Hidden in a heart-shaped box;
No-one will see it.

I love the lovely way you love the way I love my love.

The rest is private.

VII. The Future Is Not Ours To See

We can only guess,
The future is not ours to see
That's what makes it … **Fun**.

The past is long gone,
Traced in fractal river deltas.
The present is now

About to unfold,
Converging trajectories:
What could/might/will be.

There's nothing to lose;
Just one step after another.
Is there any choice?

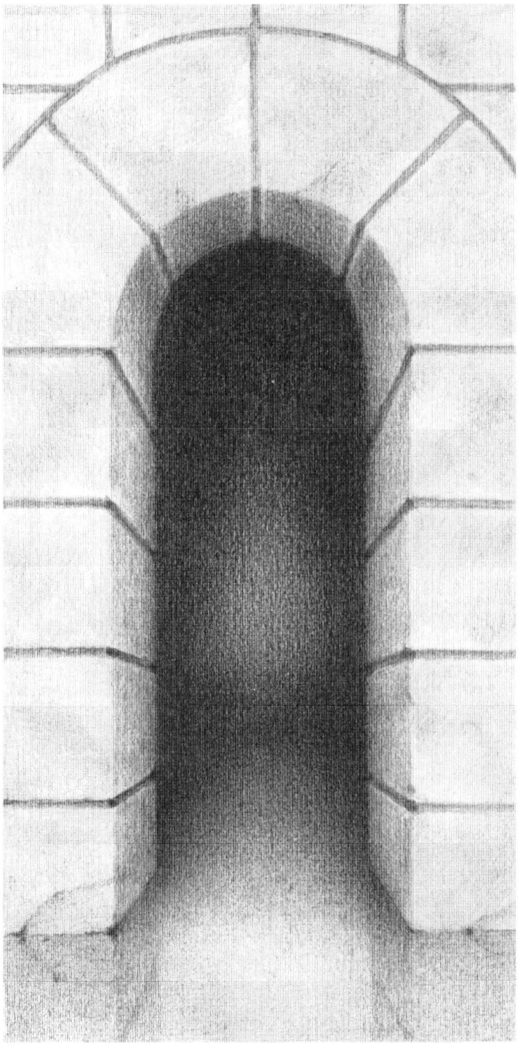

VIII. Help ... My Mandala Mutated

Sometimes what we plan goes astray and ends up as something we did not originally intend.

That isn't always a bad thing.

Projects can grow in ways that we never thought of at the beginning, a mix of luck and flexibility can be central to any successful endeavour. You just need to keep your mind open to the new possibilities and recognise the serendipity.

Of course, sometimes things become irrecoverable and lessons must be learned … that's not such a bad thing either.

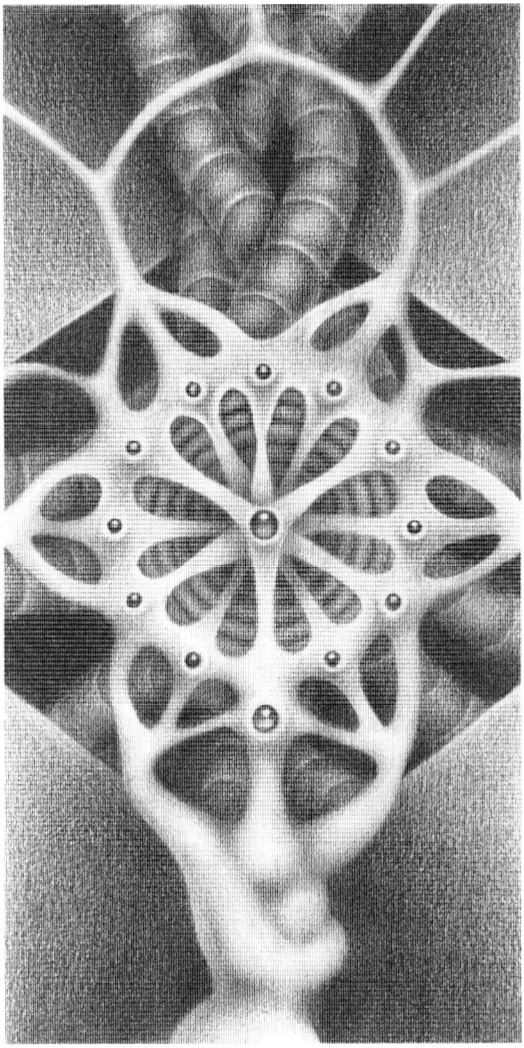

IX. Keeping Secrets

Finding the keys within
The realms of experience
There are secrets.

The effort required to keep secrets can be too much. On the one hand telling secrets can be a betrayal of trust but on the other, secrets steal the truth. Better to throw the secrets to the winds so that they can be seen and known. It avoids nasty surprises and greater betrayals in the long run.

X. It Is Inevitable

Flaking and paper dry,
This diaphanous existence
Will soon dissipate.

Life is short. Get used to it because it will soon be gone. Do what you can while you can, you never know when your faculties will be lost.

Fighting entropy?
It is inevitable;
We all fall apart.

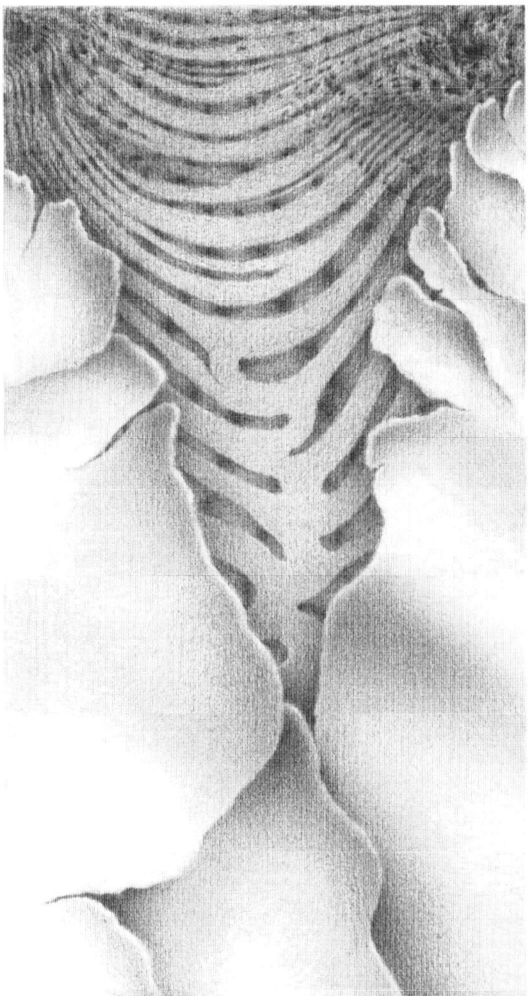

XI. Self Organisation

Perfect imperfections;
Self organisation;
It is what it is.

We build stories to make sense of our lives. We tell our experiences from a single point of view; this is only to be expected as we only inhabit ourselves. Different people can make different stories about the very same events, depending on their own needs and desires, (your story, my story and history). Which story is the most accurate is a matter for eternal debate.

Our stories define us. We are the story we write from our experiences. We should try and tell the most accurate stories whenever we can; otherwise we will always be fooling ourselves.

Stories coalesce
In ever changing patterns.
Who am I today?

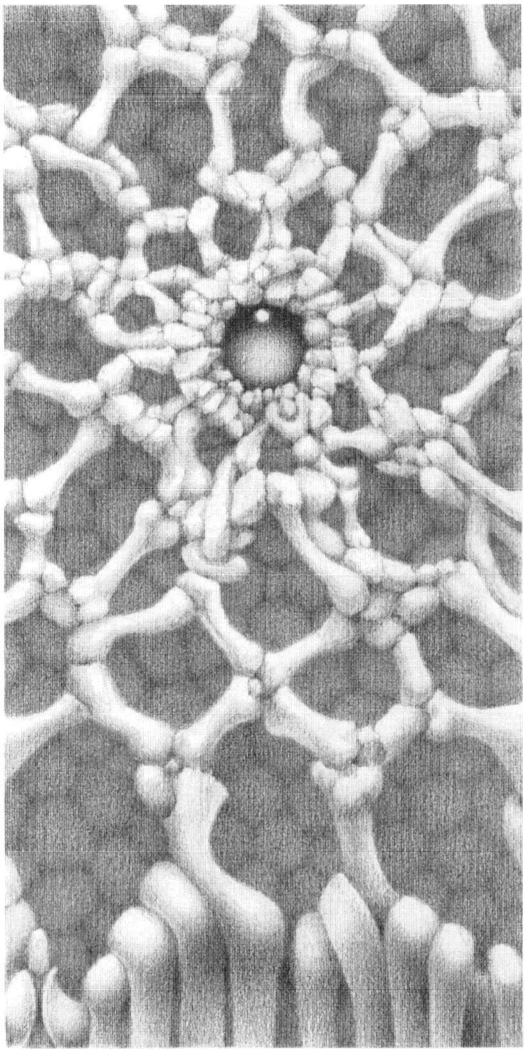

XII. Stop Making Sense

Too many details;
Random elements combine;
It doesn't make sense.

We constantly strive to find coherence in life's patterns. Sometimes, random elements coincide to give an appearance of deeper meaning, giving rise to chains of belief. Sometimes there is no pattern, there is no meaning … it all just is.

Where did this come from?
Perception and illusion;
There is no meaning.

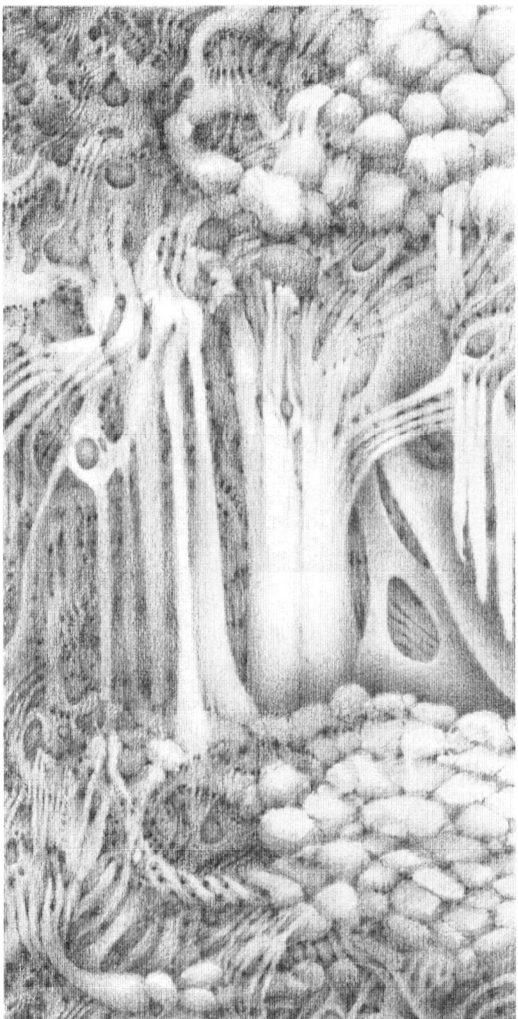

XIII. Free-Form Formation

Thoughts process in a
Doodle of convenience;
Something from nothing.

Fooling around and being unafraid of failure means that there are opportunities to have ideas and make new connections. While the number of unworkable ideas may vastly outweigh the number of useful ideas, without silly ideas there would be no useful ideas at all. Sometimes, those unworkable ideas need only a few tweaks to become really useful.

Inspiration flows;
Ideas take flight;
Play is so under-rated.

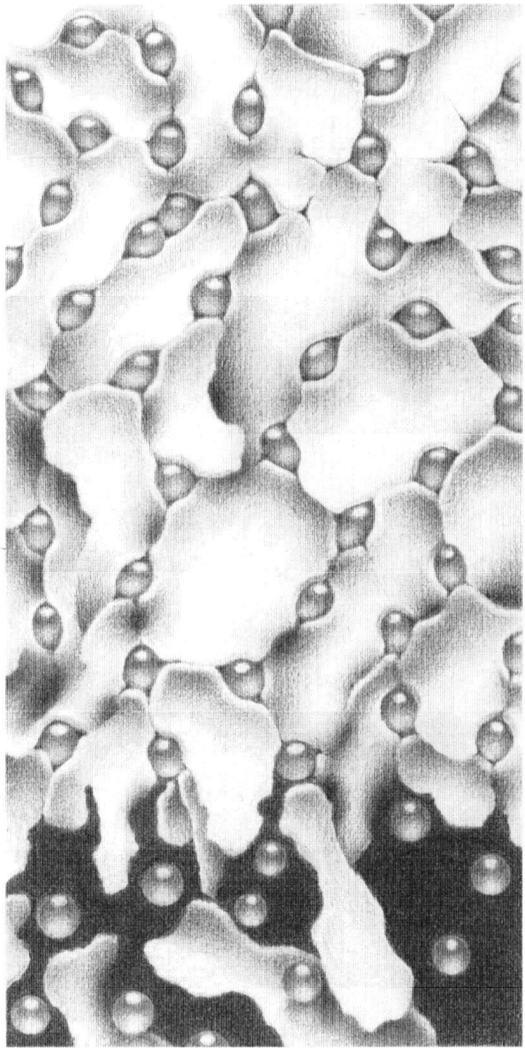

XIV. Time For Bed

Ready for bed?
My favourite time of day
To clear the mind.

There is a special point between sleep and awake that is other-worldly. It is not dreaming, yet not fully conscious. It is where ideas are free from the confines of rational thought, behaving like naughty little imps.

They are so difficult to catch.

XV. Escape Artist

Caught in the act of
Escaping the confines
And breaking the rules.

Rules are everywhere, invading everything we do. We need to know the rules, they are essential in the collective human society and obeying them is a part of life. Some rules are written in stone, (**THOU SHALT NOT KILL**), some are an unwritten consensus, (It's Rude To Stare) and some are self-imposed, (stop eating chocolate).

We all break the rules … they are made to be broken. When is it OK to break the rules? Do the rules need to be re-examined?

When is my revolutionary your terrorist?

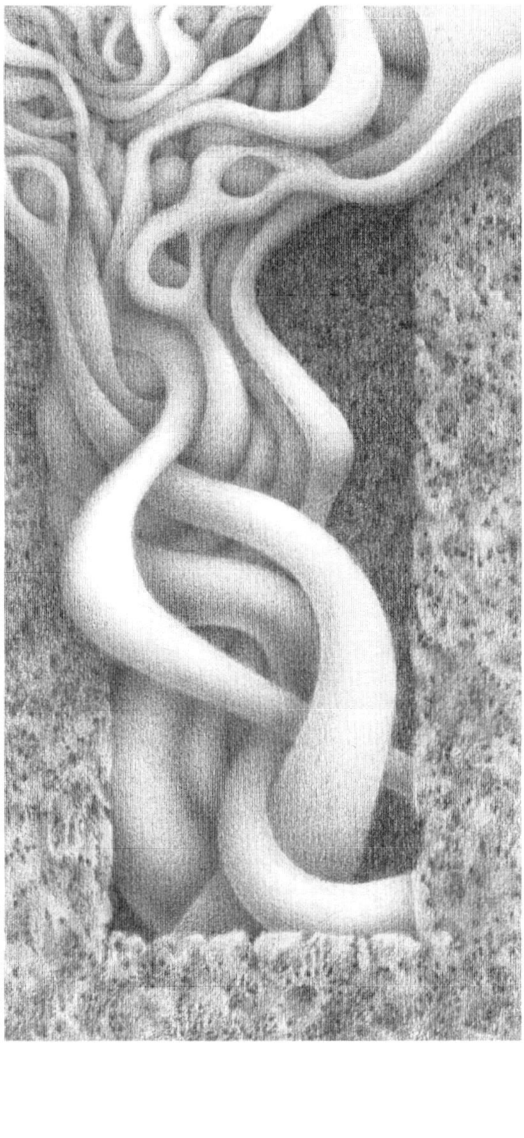

XVI. Contrasts

Hard, soft, near and far;
With darkness and light defined
The contrasts leap out.

Some things are easy to define in and of themselves. Others are harder to pin down and are more easily defined by what they are not.

Sometimes I don't really know what I am looking for … I hope I'll know what it is when I find it …

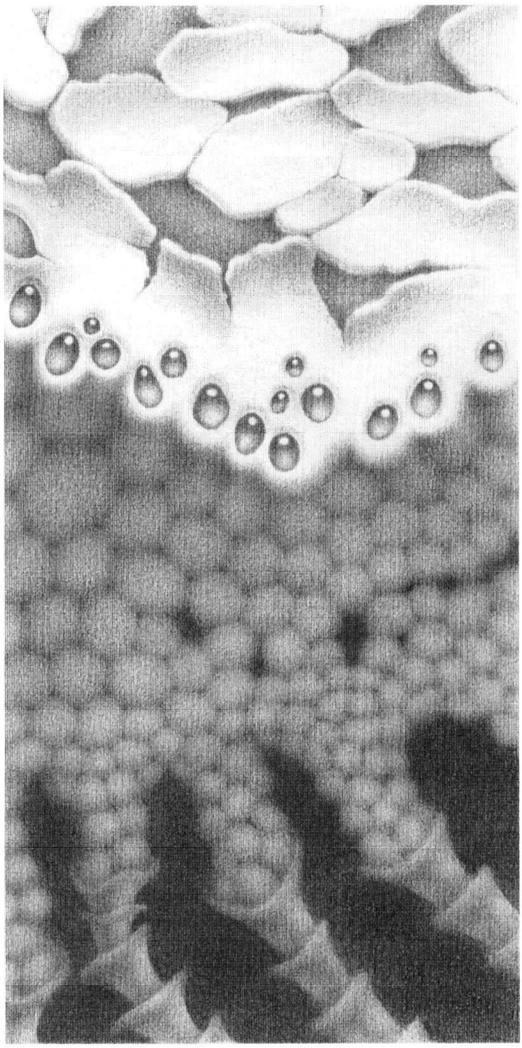

XVII. Monolithic Nocturne

Dust-dry, deserted;
A monolithic nocturne
Alone at the end.

What will be left of human existence after 100 years, or 1000 years or 100,000,000 years? What if some alien species comes across the remnants of the pyramids or the skeletal remains of cities lost in the dust? How will they decipher the clues and piece together the structure of human civilisations?

Time is a crazy concept to grasp relative to our short life spans. All that we build seems trivial in comparison with the lifetime of the universe.

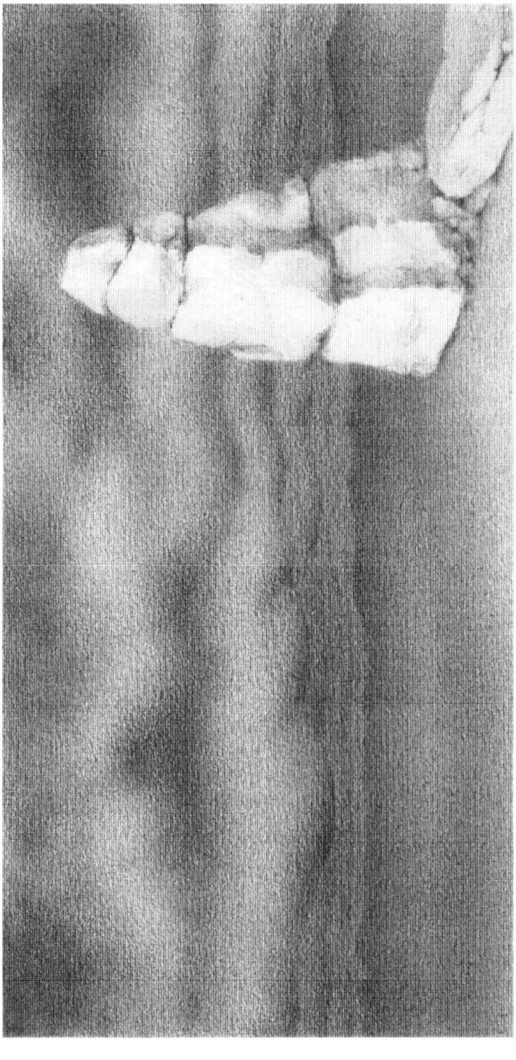

XVIII. Symbiosis

Entwined together;
A marriage of opposites;
Two halves make a whole.

Perhaps two halves can make more than a whole.

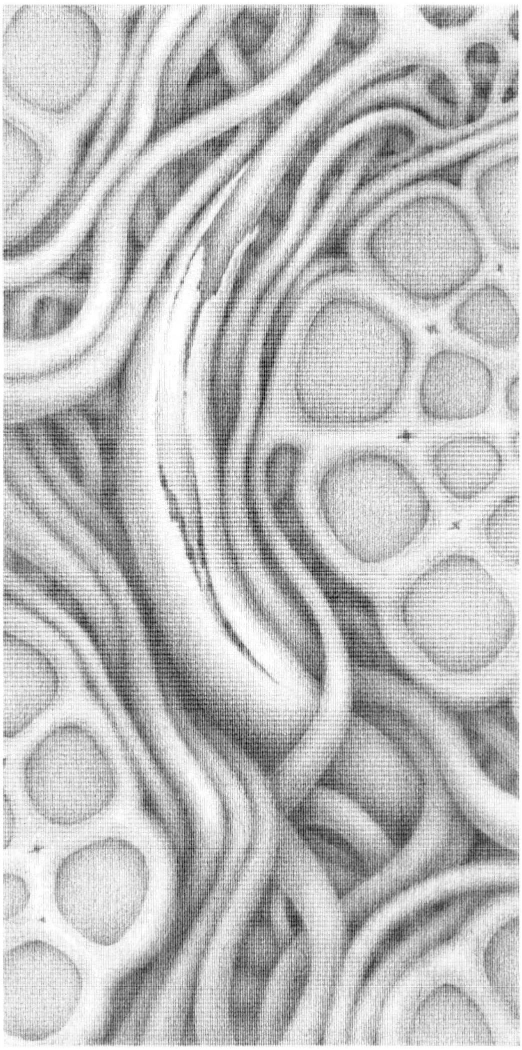

XIX. Surprising Results

Blending different forms
From across the borderlands;
New combinations.

Where different worlds meet there are opportunities for comparison and reflection. What seems mundane and everyday can be thrown into the light, to be re-examined and appreciated anew.

Collaborations, where perspectives are equally exchanged, often combine two separate visions to generate new and surprising hybrids.

Working together
With unexpected results;
An equal exchange.

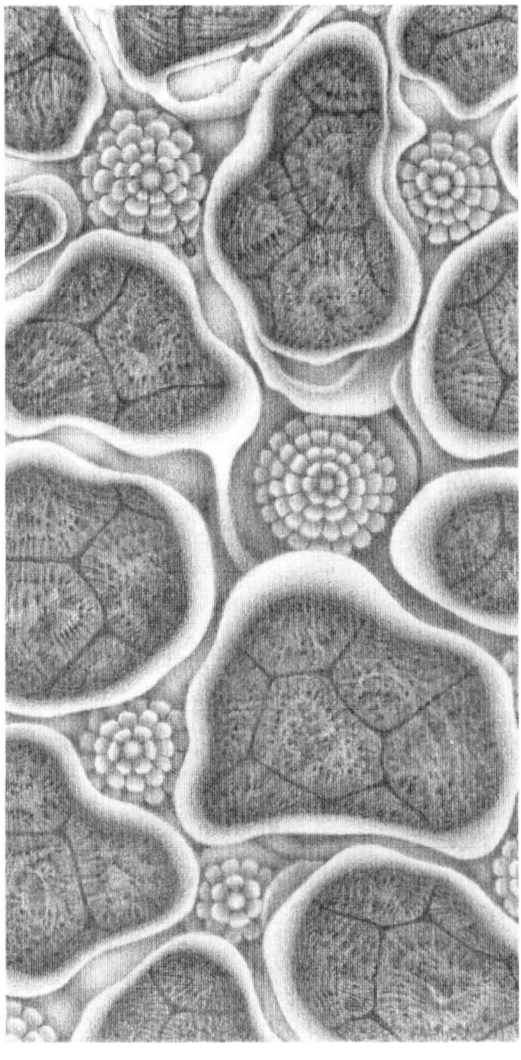

XX. Drawing By Numbers

This puzzle piece;
Is everything in its right place?
A number sequence.

We build categories and fit things (or events … or people) into boxes with labels of the closest match. I'm never sure whether the match I'm about to make is close enough to be useful or whether the categories I have designed are indeed the best possible options. Sometimes, in the light of new matches, I must make a new category and then try and work out how to best fit it into the library of those already in use. If my categories are too precise or my judgements are too strict, I may miscategorise something. There's always something that defies categorisation and ends up languishing on the floor, waiting for the day when **JUDGEMENT** can be made.

What use are these categories? Why do I feel the need to categorise? Am I not just making trouble for myself and creating divisions where, in reality, none exist?

Don't these categories speak more about me than the thing I am trying to categorise?

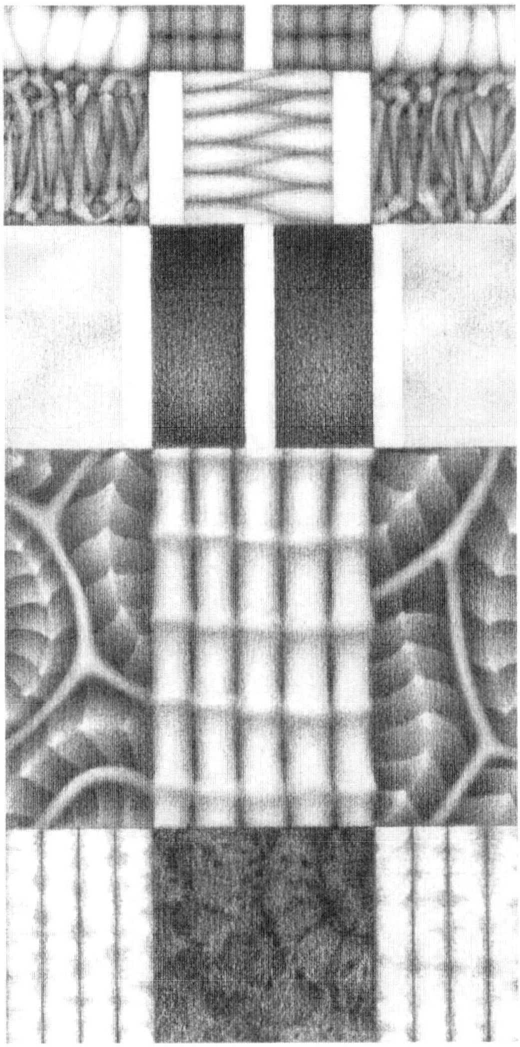

XXI. Too Alien For Words

Jostling Jelly rolls;
Too alien for words;
They defy description.

Some things are so different that they stand apart and cannot be described in any meaningful way. There are no words to define them. It is as though language has failed and we think more in terms of feelings.

How much of human consciousness depends on language and what would we be without it?

Understanding the world;
What do we really know?
Words create structure.

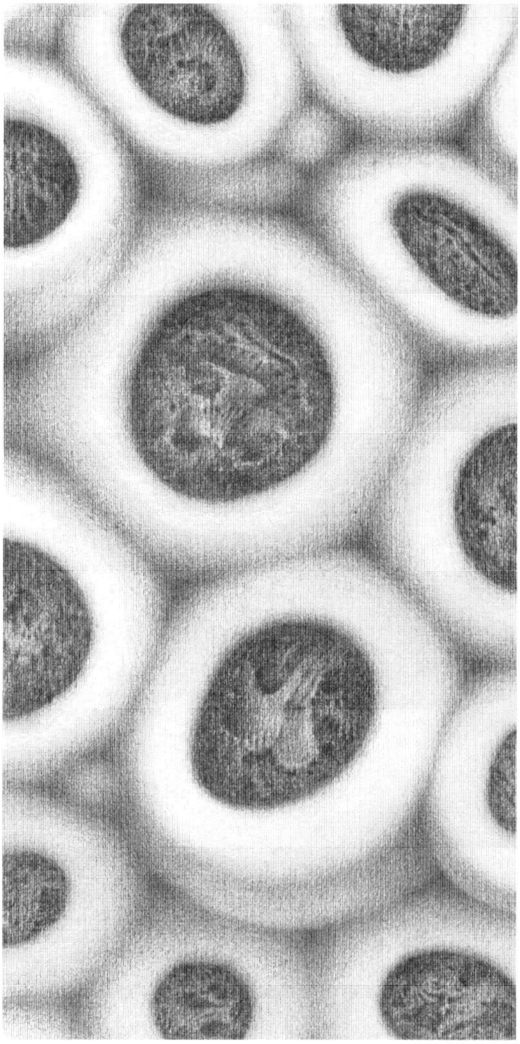

XXII. Lost In Translation

Such high hopes at first
Unravelling in each phase;
Lost in translation.

Each drawing begins with such high hopes, but each drawing becomes just a shadow of its original potential as errors and unintended things creep in.

We often have great expectations and most of the time we are disappointed; things rarely work out the way we want them to. Is it our fault for being unrealistic or does the fault lie elsewhere when our expectations are not met?

Disappointments lie
In great expectations
Beyond our control.

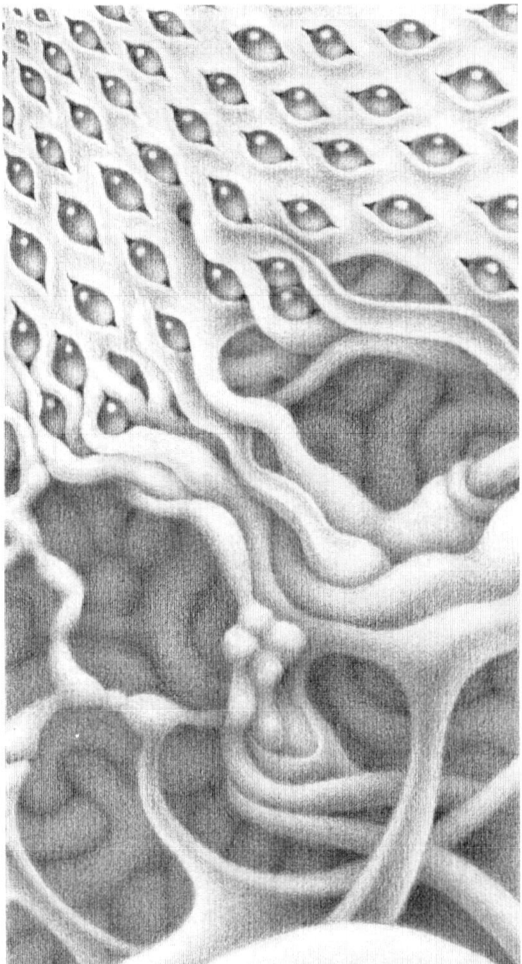

XXIII. The Wall

Hitting the wall,
Frustrating all thoughts of progress
To find a way through.

At times, all sense of progression shudders to a stubborn stop. A plateau is reached where, no matter how much effort is invested, things do not appear to evolve.

I find it best to keep going, practising my scales and waiting for the moment when some unexpected trigger opens up a way through to the next level.

Sometimes it takes a while.

At least the practise is useful.

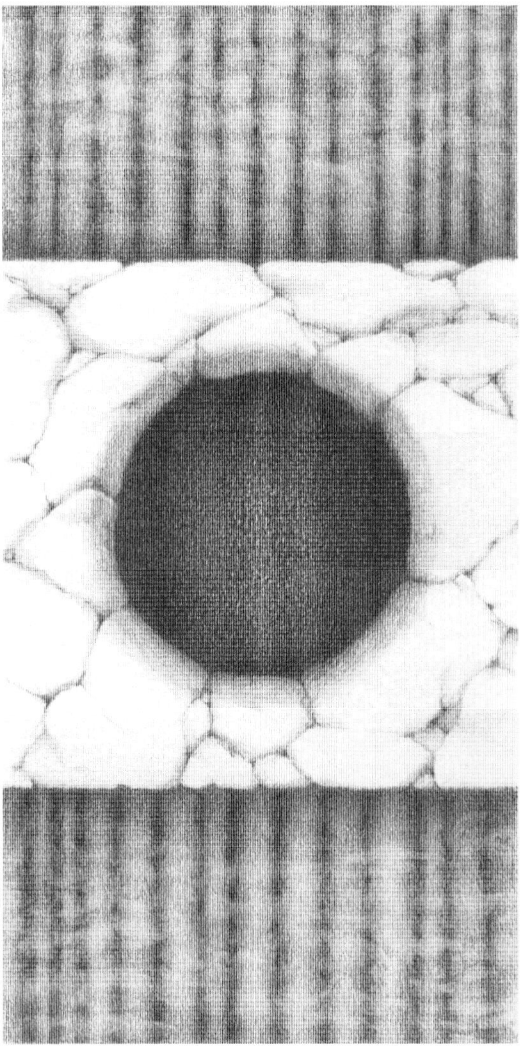

XXIV. Playing Your Cards

At the beginning
Random forces are combined;
The cards are dealt.

We, as human beings, are born with a fundamental set of genes into an environment over which we have no real control. It is up to us to play our set of cards and do the best we can. Some people are lucky and some not so lucky. We all have to play the game.

No aces up my sleeve,
Am I doing this right?
Just playing the game.

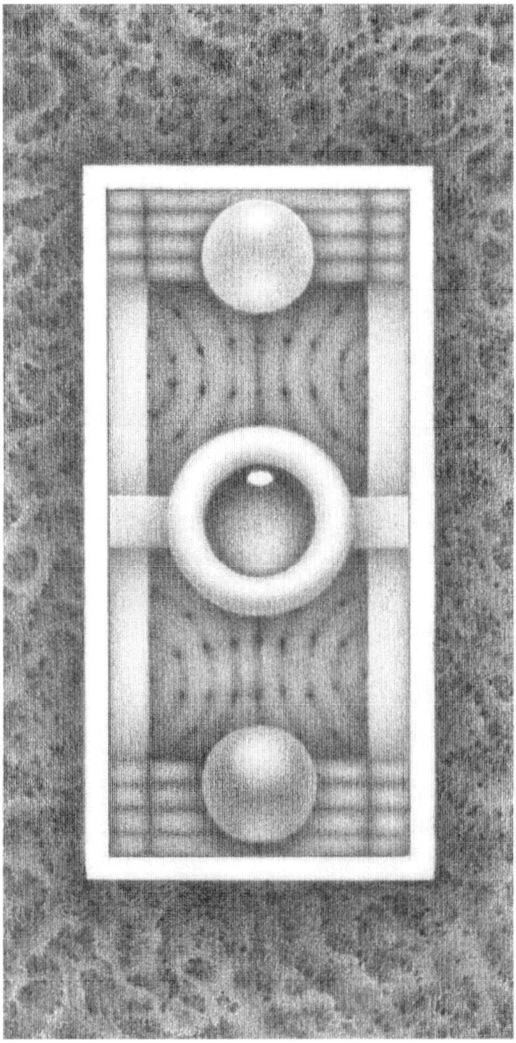

XXV. Nothing Is Perfect

Something is missing;
Secrets, lies and confessions;
Erase and replace.

Perhaps you cannot tell where it went wrong, but I know it did. I erased and replaced a section of this drawing, (as I have done secretly in another drawing but I'm not going to tell you which one), because it felt awkward.

I should not have done that; it is against the rules of this book.

Now I have confessed … I feel better.

We all make mistakes.

Seeking forgiveness,
A hole in the composition;
Nothing is perfect.

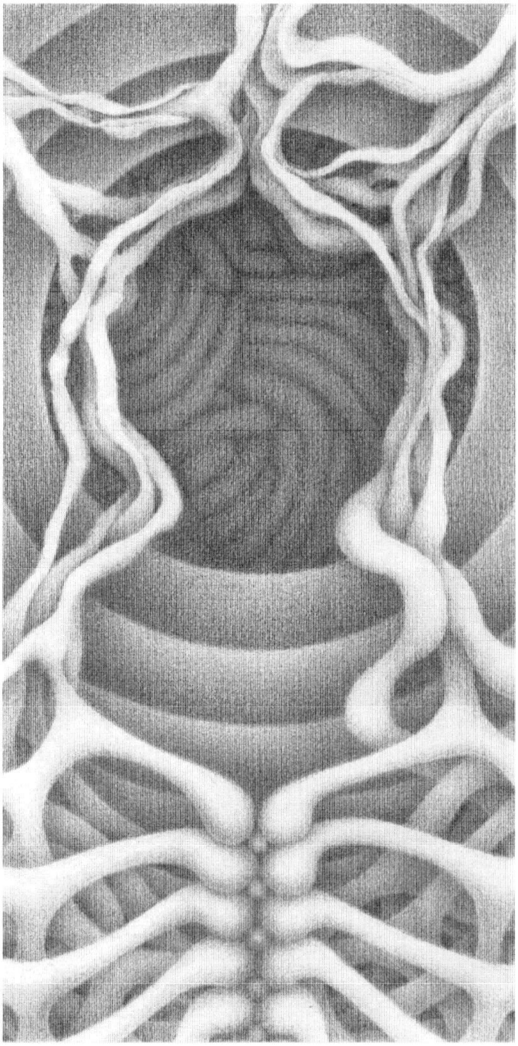

XXVI. Cracking Up

Cracking under stress,
Just holding it together;
Be nice to yourself.

Stresses can come in many forms. Some are temporary, like passing tests or travelling to work. Others are more insidious, like trying to be something we are not or trying to please everyone. That's not to say that we shouldn't try to be a better person - just that we don't need to be a different person.

We should be nice to ourselves and accept that, at the end of the day, we are who we are and that is all we have.

We should celebrate other people for who they are not for who we want them to be.

XXVII. So Ugly, It's Cute

Just hanging around
To be appreciated;
One of a kind.

We can trace our origins back over billions of years of evolutionary reproduction. That we exist and experience life is, in itself, a huge success: so many potential lives didn't make it this far. Everyone has a mix of talent and experience that is unique; everyone has something of value to offer.

Are you the best **YOU**
You can possibly be?
We are all unique.

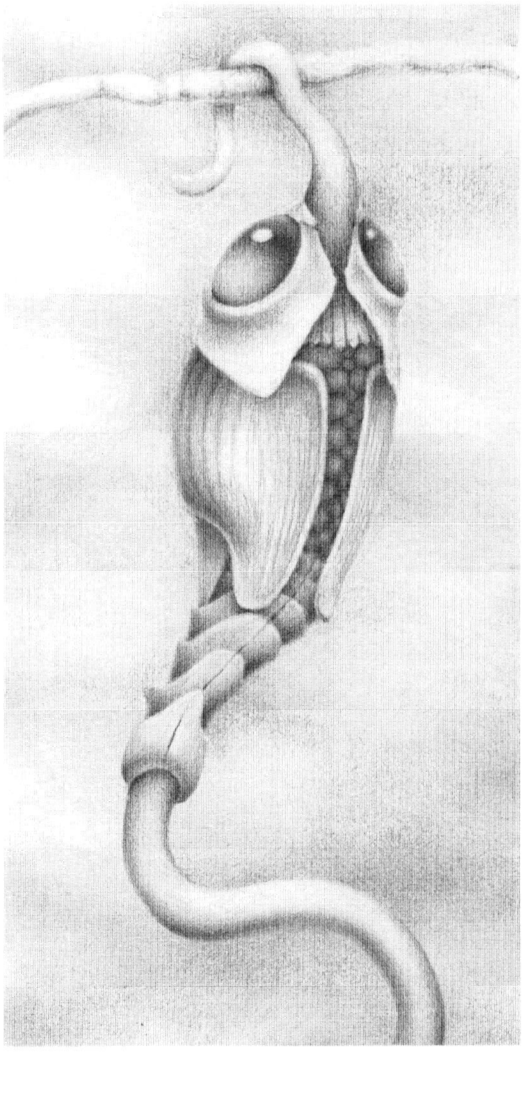

XXVIII. Sex On Paper

Uncensored, explicit sex on paper.

How would you know if I hadn't told you?

We'll just keep it as our little secret shall we ...

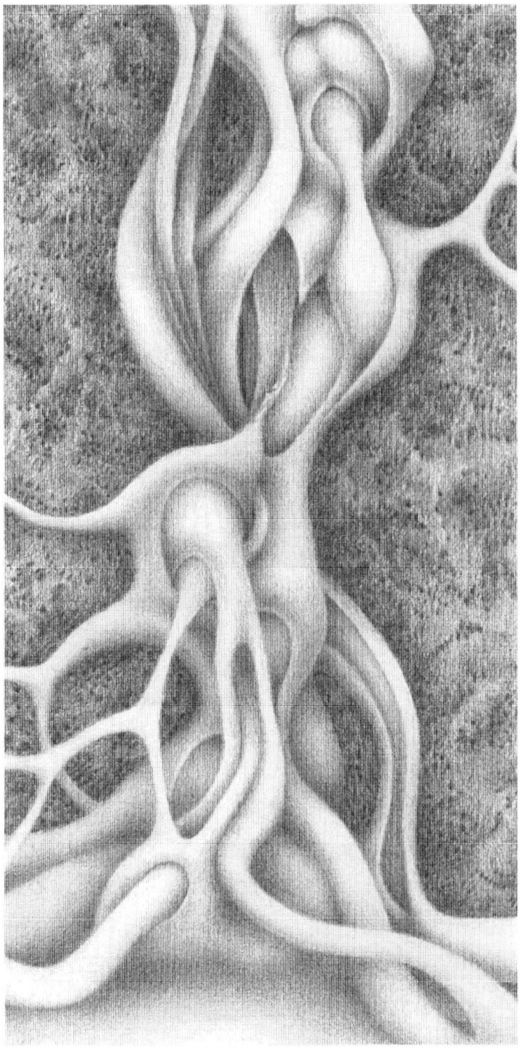

XXIX. Simple Complexity

Or should that be complex simplicity?

The pursuit of knowledge is a marvellous thing. At first one learns the information and thinks one has complete grasp of the facts. Then one learns where the facts came from and finds that there are assumptions and caveats. Then one places things into context and realises that there are many interpretations and we need new facts to distinguish between all the possible conclusions.

Many people see factual knowledge as resolute and insoluble, yet so often, what we think we know turns out to be wrong. Besides, however much has been learned, there is an infinite amount of **STUFF** still to understand and questions that have not yet been asked so that really, in the grand scheme of things, we actually know very little.

Re-wiring the neurons;
Information is not knowledge;
Knowledge is not wisdom.

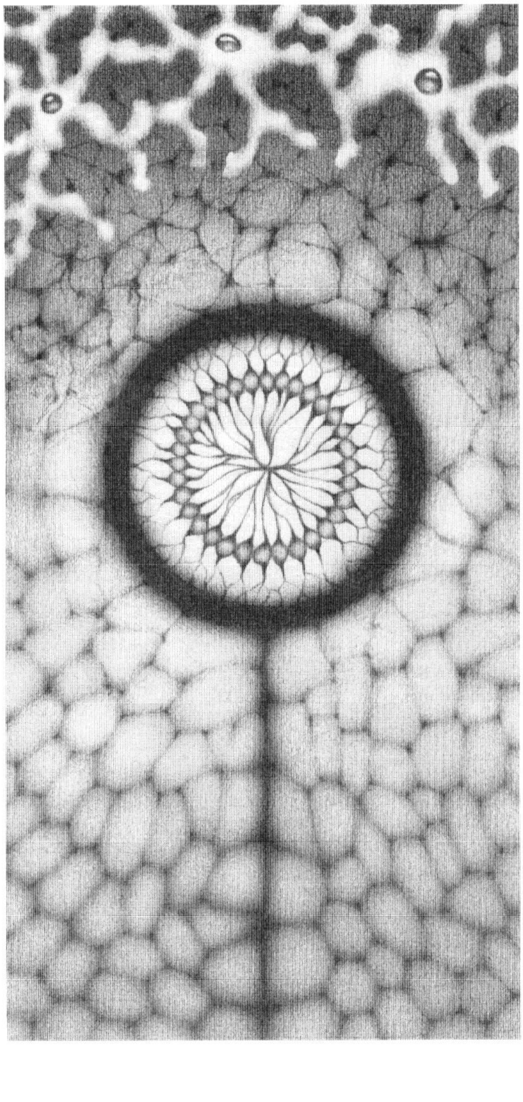

XXX. Parasites; They're Not Pretty

A mass of threads in
Parasitic entanglement;
They're not pretty.

Doubts and insecurities can lead to a sense of helplessness, sapping our energies. These parasites need to be recognised and dealt with. It's not always that easy to spot the point at which they take hold and the best medicine is to seek good companions that take our attentions somewhere more positive.

We should all be prepared to diagnose these parasites in others and be ready with the appropriate medication.

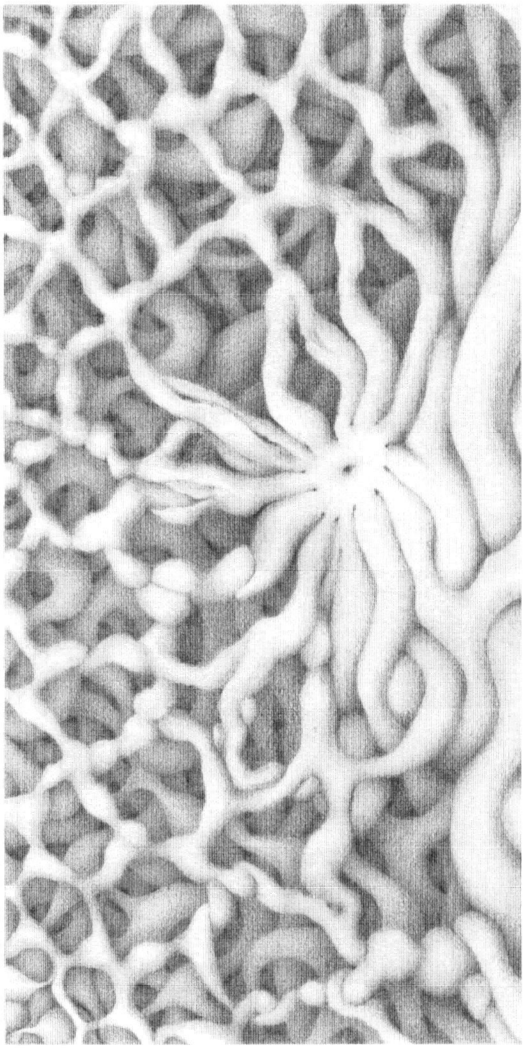

XXXI. Layers

Different layers
Competing with each other;
Who will be the winner?

People sometimes compete to be the best. While we can agree on how to measure who is fastest over 100m, what measurements can we use to decide if one person is better than another? Does everyone agree the rules beforehand or are we allowed to pick those measures that favour our own requirements as and when we feel like it?

How can we tell who is better than who and what does it all mean anyway?

What is the prize for "Best Person"?

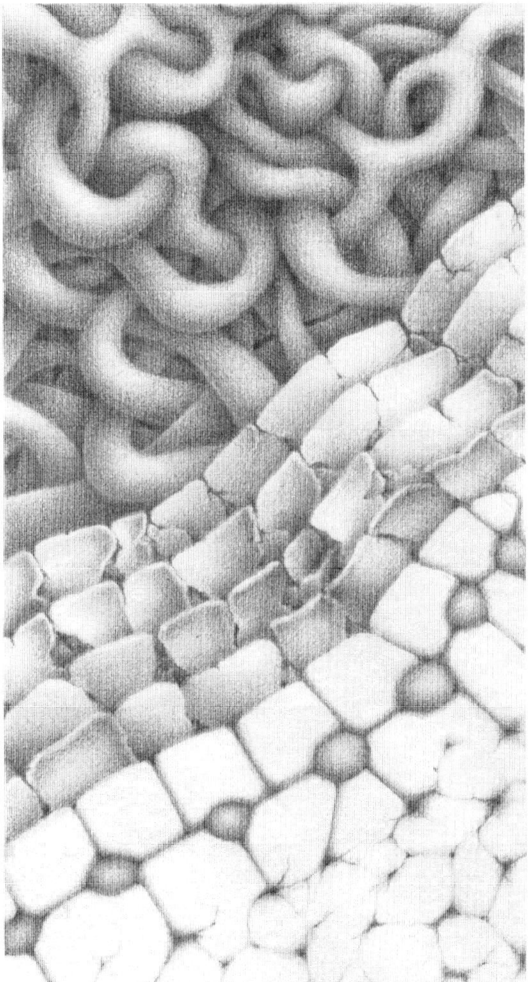

XXXII. Foundations Of Balance

In the balancing act
Everything plays its part;
Strengths and weaknesses.

It is funny how our strengths in one situation become weaknesses as the situation changes. It all seems to depend on perspective and relativity.

Life is a paradox in so many ways.

A cursory glance
Or attention to detail?
It's all relative.

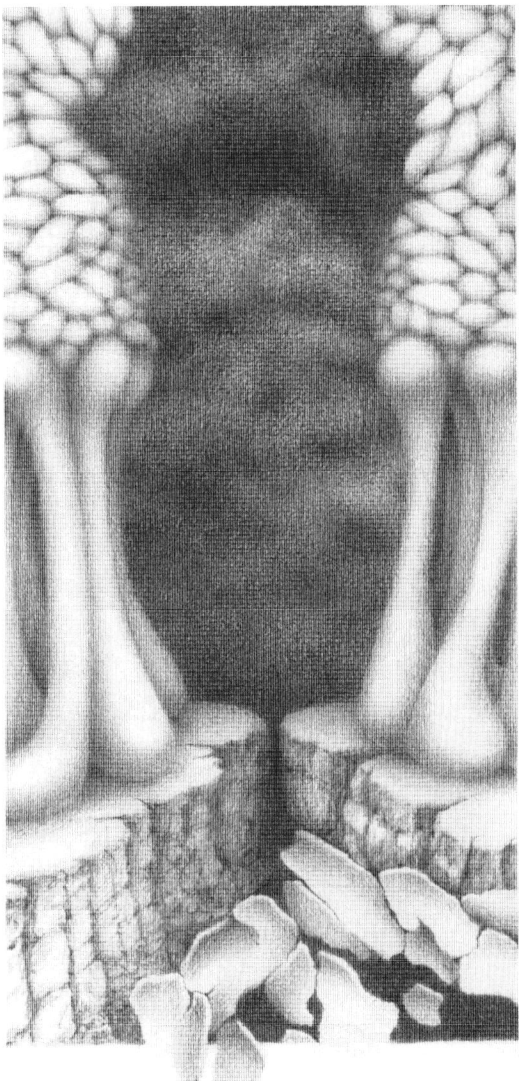

XXXIII. Growth And Decay

Embryonic life forms
Creating new structures;
Growth involves decay.

Throughout the natural world there are predators and prey. Energy and matter interchange and disorganisation from decay become organised into new growth.

Sometimes an endeavour consumes resources, becoming bloated and useless; best to pick it apart and build something new.

Everything gets recycled eventually.

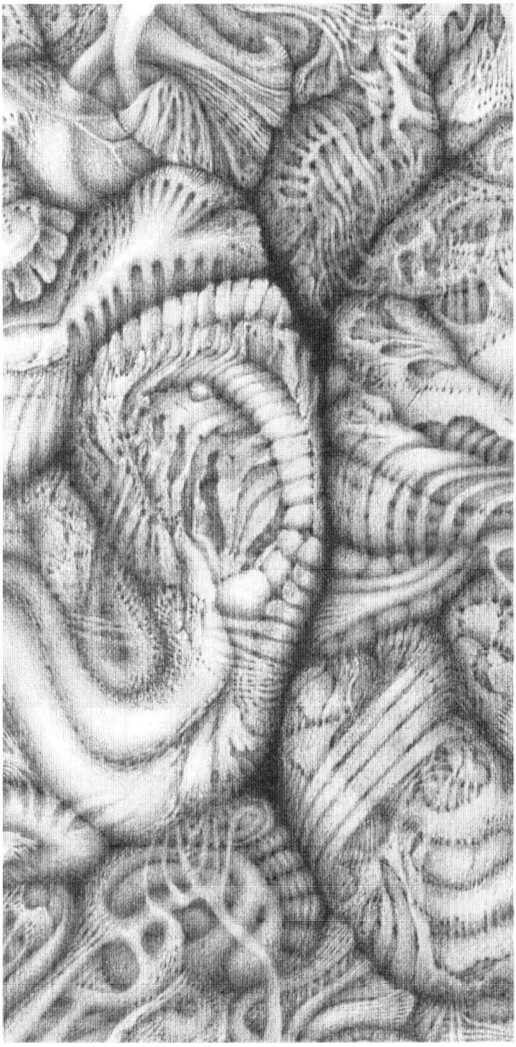

XXXIV. Things May Not Be As They Seem

Missing some details;
Things may not be as they seem
At first impression.

We all make assumptions about life without really thinking. So much so, that these assumptions can become invisible unless we make a conscious effort to identify them. We should all reflect on our first impressions and constantly question whether our prejudices really are justified.

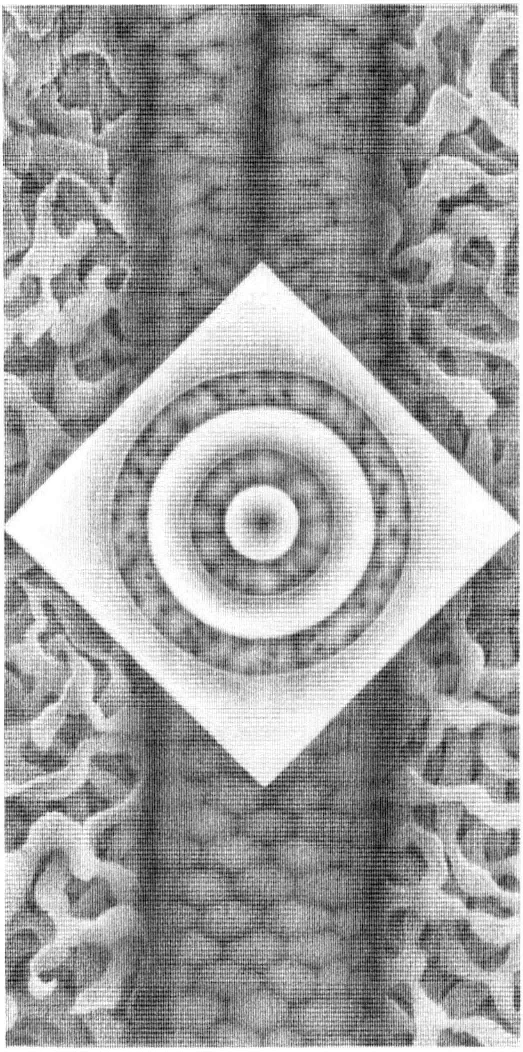

XXXV. I Started … So I Finished

Journeys combine
Past losses with future rewards;
Ends and beginnings.

Here, at the end of the book, there is a sense of a battle won. It might not be the greatest of achievements … but I have at least finished … if only because I began.

Now it is time to begin something new.

ACKNOWLEDGEMENTS

Special thanks to Neil, Ian and Brenda for proofreading and all the love and support.

With much love to family and friends.

www.salhunter.deviantart.com

www.sallyhunter.co.uk